Henley on Th

PHOEBE TAPLIN

For many people Henley on Thames is synonymous with its Royal Regatta, but this historic town offers so much more than just rowing. Built between the winding river and the wooded Chiltern Hills, Henley has been part of a beautiful landscape for more than a millennium. It was a busy medieval port, a vital 18th-century coaching town and home to several industries, including malting, brewing, glass-making and boat-building.

The Royal Regatta, the world's most famous rowing festival, began in 1839 and is now just one of Henley's many annual explosions of boats and colourful costumes. The town also hosts numerous celebrations each year of music, literature, theatre, food and sport. The winter months are busy too, with fairs and markets, concerts, conferences and fun runs.

Henley's rich and varied architecture ranges from half-timbered cottages to neo-Gothic castles. The town has inspired engineers, artists, writers and musicians. Films and television serials, including *The Social Network* and *Downton Abbey*, have used Henley and its surroundings as a setting for their productions.

There are natural treasures here as well as cultural ones. The riverbanks are abundant in flowers and birdlife; the red kites that were once almost extinct are now a common sight in the skies above Henley. Visitors to the award-winning River & Rowing Museum can see grey herons, otters and other river-dwelling creatures. Here too are artefacts discovered in the depths of the Thames that tell the story of human settlements along the river, the crafts and traders rooted in its history. Other collections include the history of rowing, from ancient warfare to competitive sport – and much more besides.

Enjoy exploring!

Hobbs of Henley's paddle steamer.

Historic Henley

Henley on Thames has been a market town for nearly ten centuries. Archaeological discoveries, like a hoard of golden coins found in a field near the town, provide intriguing hints about life in the area another thousand years before that. The British Iron Age coins, decorated with a three-tailed horse, were buried in a hollow flint nodule together with two Roman coins. Excavations have uncovered Roman villas and farms in the area, including one underneath Waitrose supermarket.

Medieval Henley was an important inland port, sending timber, grain and malt downstream to London. As trade expanded, the town grew. Along many of Henley's streets you can still see early buildings, such as the 14th-century Old Bell Inn on Bell Street and the 15th-century Baltic Cottage on the riverside corner of Friday Street. The weekly market, still held on Thursdays, is likely to date from the town's earliest years. Local craftsmen sold goods made from wood, metal, leather and textiles.

Above: The medieval Chantry House is situated behind St Mary's Church.

The Civil War and Beyond

Henley was caught in the middle of the Civil War, half way between royalist Oxford, where Charles I had fled, and Oliver Cromwell's parliamentary forces in the capital. The King's troops damaged local mansions and the old wooden bridge. The Speaker of the House of Commons, William Lenthal, whose refusal to help the King sparked the war in 1642, was born in Henley at 44 Hart Street. He told Charles I: 'I have neither eyes to see, nor tongue to speak, but as the House is pleased to direct me, whose servant I am here.'

Travel and trade increased again after the Civil War and maps in James Ogilby's 1675 book *Britannia* charted the road from London to Oxford via Henley. The town developed as a crucial staging post for coaches in the 18th century; the present bridge was constructed and

Below: The Henley Hoard: these 2,000-year-old gold coins can be seen at the River & Rowing Museum.

Above: Fragments from a 'time capsule' discovered in Henley Park and dating from 1731, displayed at the River & Rowing Museum.

Left: The Red Lion Hotel, originally built in 1531 to accommodate the craftsmen building St Mary's Church.

Below: Henley has more than 300 listed buildings.

wealthy merchants built handsome houses from local brick, like the mansion known as 'Countess Gardens' at 88 Bell Street, the riverside Old Rectory, and the 'new Town Hall', erected in 1787, though since replaced.

The glamour of Henley's late 18th-century social scene is revealed in the diaries of Caroline Lybbe Powys, including entertaining descriptions of an impromptu royal visit, a glittering 'gala week', water parties, and local balls where she danced all night. She also praises the new theatre, which opened in 1805.

More Modern Times

In the 19th century, rail travel took over from coaches and barges and the town became a fashionable resort, epitomized by the famous Regatta. A series of new guidebooks promoted Henley's scenic charms and by 1896 there were 28 passenger trains arriving daily from London all year round. Emily Climenson's *Guide to Henley* describes the Regatta as 'the world's water picnic' with 'the kaleidoscopic glow of colour and form, represented by every variety of craft', and 'stalwart men, brilliant in their coloured flannels'.

Local businesses grew and flourished, including the well-established Brakspear and Sons brewery, dating from the 18th century, which built malthouses on New Street in 1899. Boat-builders, among them the Hobbs family, were making everything from punts to steam launches. New boathouses, boatyards, clubs and restaurants began to line the riverbanks. Old coaching inns like the Red Lion became fancy hotels and a grandstand for viewing the Regatta appeared in the grounds of Phyllis Court.

The town continued to expand and to develop as a tourist destination. Modern Henley still attracts walkers, shoppers, music-lovers and, of course, boaters. The 1936 *Salter's Guide to the Thames* mentions the golf courses, the 'delightful walks and drives' through river or woodland scenery, and the chance to play tennis or bowls in the public riverside gardens at Mill Meadows, now also home of the River & Rowing Museum. The Museum celebrates the town's history and world-famous sporting heritage while the pioneering architecture and interactive exhibits embrace the 21st century.

Above: The old brewery building in New Street.

The River

As the name suggests, Henley on Thames has always been intimately connected to the river, both as a trading port and crossing point.

The Thames flows for more than 200 miles (320km) from Gloucestershire to the North Sea; it has traditionally been crossed by numerous bridges and ferries and, more recently, by tunnels, a cable car and the Thames Flood Barrier.

The handsome, five-arched Henley Bridge replaced an earlier wooden bridge in 1786. The older bridge, first built around the 12th century, was damaged in the Civil War and finally swept away in a flood in 1774.

The River & Rowing Museum has examples of all kinds of boats, from a 5th-century Saxon canoe to those used in modern-day Olympics. Steam launches, sailing punts, royal barges and many other vessels have floated or motored through Henley.

Harry Hobbs founded the boat hire firm Hobbs and Sons (now Hobbs of Henley Ltd) in 1870 and the company moved to its current location, at the end of Station Road, 30 years later. In 1990 they commissioned the luxurious *New Orleans* paddle steamer, which has become a town landmark. The hire fleet, which includes elegant river buses sporting teak panelling and panoramic windows, and traditional open launches for the Regatta's umpires, is now the largest on the Thames. The Hobbs family has lived locally since medieval times and has given Henley three mayors and two Royal Watermen.

Towpath and Riverside Buildings

Along the river to the north are rows of boathouses and grand waterside estates. The towpath beside the rowing course over the bridge is restricted during the Regatta or when the river floods, but otherwise makes a lovely stroll (about 3 miles/5km for the round trip). If you choose to walk past the places mentioned below, you will need to cross the bridge from the town centre and turn left along the Thames Path near the Leander Club.

Phyllis Court

Phyllis Court, now a private club enjoying the best view of the Regatta, is in Henley's north-eastern corner. It can trace its history back to 1301 when it was the local manor house, and has welcomed several royal visitors, from Queen Anne of Denmark in 1604 to HM Queen Elizabeth II.

Fawley Court

There was already a manor at Fawley Court by 1066. Parliamentarian Bulstrode Whitelocke lived in the house in the 17th century, when Royalist troops attacked it. Colonel William Freeman, a merchant and sugar plantation owner, built the present house in 1684 in the

Below: Henley Bridge. There has been a crossing place over the Thames at this spot for many centuries.

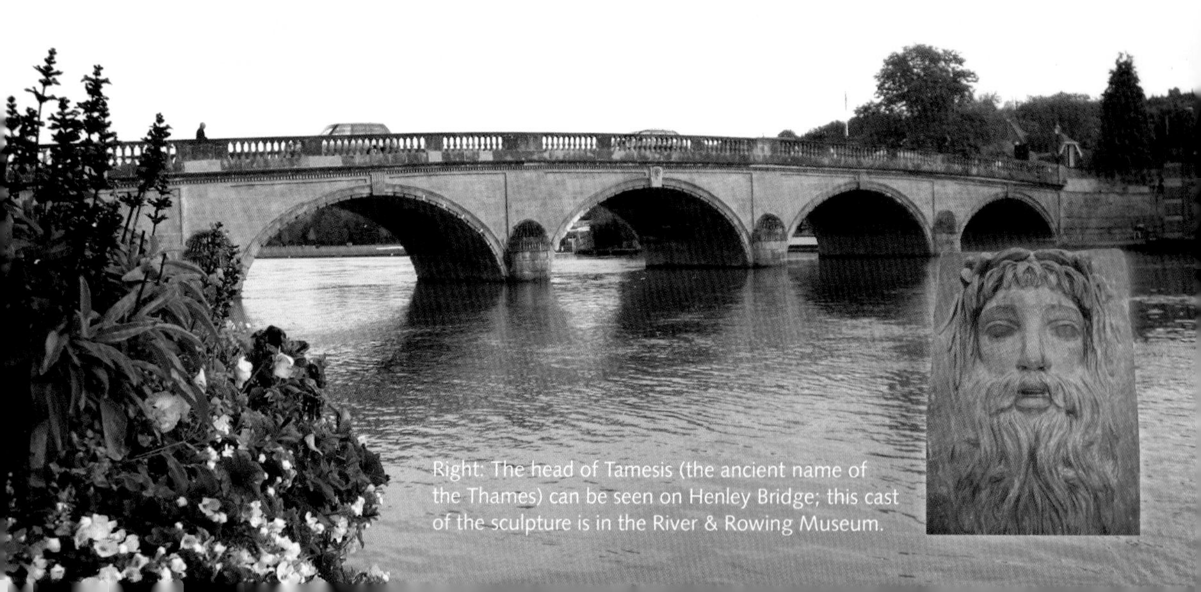

Right: The head of Tamesis (the ancient name of the Thames) can be seen on Henley Bridge; this cast of the sculpture is in the River & Rowing Museum.

Above: The summer house on Temple Island. The Royal Regatta course runs upstream from here to Poplar Point.

Above: Fawley Court.

style popularized by Christopher Wren. The Scottish railway engineer William Mackenzie, who bought the red-brick Fawley Court in the 19th century, built the ornamental waterway through the garden to the Thames. After the Second World War (when the house was requisitioned for training military intelligence), the Polish Marian Fathers ran a boys' school here.

Remenham

The scattered village of Remenham has a Norman church, a boathouse and a number of converted barns. Caleb Gould, Hambleden's lock-keeper for half a century from 1777, is buried in the churchyard; his gravestone reads: 'This world's a jest, and all things show it; I thought so once, but now I know it.'

Temple Island

The architect James Wyatt designed the elegant summer house on Temple Island in 1771, commissioned as a fishing lodge by Sambrooke Freeman, then owner of Fawley Court. It is now the starting point for the Royal Regatta.

Greenlands

As the Thames curves eastwards, the white mansions of Greenlands, north along the river, come into view. Greenlands saw fighting in the Civil War as the Roundheads besieged a Royalist stronghold here. There are cannon balls from the site in the River & Rowing Museum. The current house dates from the 19th century and W.H. Smith, the stationer, bought it in 1872; it is described in Jerome K. Jerome's *Three Men in a Boat* as the 'river residence of my newsagent – a quiet unassuming old gentleman …'. The family sold it to Henley Business School (now part of the University of Reading) more than 60 years ago.

Hambleden Lock and Village

The first-ever Oxford and Cambridge Boat Race in 1829 ran between Hambleden Lock and Henley Bridge; Oxford won, and the boat itself can be seen in the River & Rowing Museum.

There has been a mill at Hambleden Lock since the 11th century. From here, walkers can cross and go on to Hambleden village, or turn right along a track, perhaps visit the Flower Pot pub at Aston, and head back to Henley via the woods and lanes around Remenham. Alternatively, a bus runs regularly from Mill End (near Hambleden Lock) back to Henley.

Above: Greenlands.

Nature & Conservation

The Thames and its surroundings are rich in wildlife and in recent years the water quality has improved, bringing back species including salmon and otters. Conservationists have also worked to protect historic man-made structures along the river, like locks and bridges.

Marsh Meadows

Beyond Mill Meadows that border the River & Rowing Museum, bright yellow kingcups flower in Marsh Meadows in early spring; snake's head fritillaries, with their delicate checkerboard pattern, bloom in April; irises, willow herb, meadowsweet and purple loosestrife make a colourful summertime display. Swans, geese, mallards, coots, moorhens and elegant great crested grebes can be seen all year round; black-headed gulls and cormorants appear in winter.

Marsh Lock

Marsh Lock, upstream from Henley, has been operating here since at least the 13th century; a charming painting by Jan Siberechts in the River & Rowing Museum depicts it in the 17th century.

Marsh Lock is unusually placed on the other side of the river from the towpath; the long wooden bridge connecting walkers with the lock island makes it unique on the Thames. Until 1773 this was a flash lock, with mills for corn and paper on each side of the river. Part of the weir would be removed and boats carried through on the resulting 'flash' of water. Boats going upstream had to be dragged. The modern weir has fish ladders to help the trout, pike, eel and perch swim against the current.

The Thames Path

The Thames Path follows the river from its muddy source in the Cotswolds, through town and country, to Greenwich and beyond. The stretches around Henley are particularly idyllic. It is 3 miles (5km) upstream to the village of Shiplake, passing Marsh Lock. The path leaves the riverbank to skirt round the big houses on the edge of the village; following the signs will bring walkers to the welcoming Baskerville Arms next to Shiplake station, a short train ride back to Henley.

Below: Marsh Lock.

The Sport of Rowing

The lovely sweep of straight water between Henley Bridge and Temple Island stretches for 1 mile 550 yards (2.1km). It is perfect for racing and was used for the 1908 and 1948 Olympics.

Royal Regatta

From one afternoon's fun in 1839, the Henley Royal Regatta has grown into a five-day competition and social gathering over the first weekend in July. It gained the title 'Royal' in 1851, distinguishing it from Henley's other, totally separate, regattas like the Women's in June and the Town and Visitors' in August.

The Royal Regatta is a world-famous sporting event during which the river fills with different sized boats. Meanwhile, bunting-decked buildings and crowds in striped blazers or summer dresses turn the town into a colourful party. Only two boats race in each heat, meaning that busy days might see nearly 100 races, with one starting every five minutes.

The architect Terry Farrell, famous for London's M16 Headquarters and Charing Cross Station, won prizes for the design of the Royal Regatta Headquarters in 1986. The building echoes the boathouses it replaced, but adds bright colours and classical motifs to produce an iconic Henley landmark.

Below: Henley Royal Regatta: its first royal patron was Prince Albert, Queen Victoria's consort.

Rowing Clubs

Just north of the bridge, the Leander Club is one of the world's oldest and most successful rowing clubs. Founded in London in the early 19th century, it moved to Henley and the current clubhouse was built in 1897. Its members have won more than 100 Olympic medals; sporting heroes including Steve Redgrave and Matthew Pinsent, James Cracknell, Steve Williams and Pete Reed trained here and it continues to inspire and coach new champions. On 1 January 2013 the club elected double-Olympic-silver medallist Debbie Flood as its first female captain.

The world-famous Leander is just one of many different kinds of local rowing and water-sports clubs. Others include: Henley Rowing Club, founded in 1839 and taking part in the first Henley Regatta that year; Upper Thames Rowing Club, created by husband and wife team Peter and Diane Sutherland in 1963; and Henley Dragons, founded in 1991, whose teams of paddlers race colourful, dragon-themed fibre-glass boats, urged on by a drummer.

Below: Leander Club logo.

River & Rowing Museum

Henley's award-winning River & Rowing Museum is a great place to start or end a visit to the town, with its interactive galleries, changing exhibitions, cafe, shop and wildlife garden.

Above: The River & Rowing Museum is housed in this award-winning building on the banks of the Thames.

Schwarzenbach International Rowing Gallery

The Rowing Gallery charts the history of the sport from ancient Greek triremes to the modern Olympics. Visitors can see the boat that won the first-ever Boat Race in 1829, along with the one in which Steve Redgrave won his fifth gold at the Sydney Games in 2000, plus Olympic medals and torches from 1908 to 2012. A model of the Regatta course highlights landmarks like Temple Island and Fawley Court, with comments on associated sporting records. Live footage and documentaries showcase the drama of rowing.

River Gallery

Every aspect of the Thames is explored in the River Gallery: birds, mammals, fish and their environment, and archaeological treasures dredged from the murky past. Redesigned to highlight links with other world waterways, the displays cover everything from the river's geological formation to barges and bridges. The collections include lock-keepers' caps and valves from the Thames Barrier. From eel traps and stuffed trout to log boats and life jackets, here is the Thames as you have never seen it before.

Invesco Perpetual Henley Gallery

Local history is the theme of the Henley Gallery, enhanced by thousands of original objects along with films and pictures. Stone Age axes and broken Civil War swords illustrate the more violent aspects of the town's story, while examples of George Ravenscroft's lead glassware and brass taps from Brakspear barrels represent the rich and varied industrial past.

Among many curious exhibits are the ancient Henley Hoard of gold coins and a 'time capsule' of china and glass buried in 1731 by John Freeman of Fawley Court under a mound in the grounds of nearby Henley Park. Unearthed two centuries later, Freeman had included an explanation of the burial (scratched

Above: The Rowing Gallery.

in Latin using diamond on a broken pane of glass) 'so that, if perchance at some time curious posterity should examine this old rubbish, it may find something to give pleasure, and perhaps profit …'.

The collections include Henley-related works by numerous artists. Flemish landscape painter Jan Siberechts produced several local views, including a magnificent canvas owned by the Museum showing Henley from the Wargrave Road in 1698. This picture shows a wealth of historical detail: a log-laden barge passing through Marsh Lock, the smoking chimneys of the malt kilns and the timber-framed waterfront houses.

Frederick Watts' 1830 oil painting presents slow barges near Henley in the atmospheric style of Constable; Raoul Dufy's fauvist watercolour, *Regatta 1950*, has characteristically vibrant blues and impressionistic bustle.

The Wind in the Willows

Accompanied by an audio guide, a series of beautiful 3D models on the ground floor bring to life Kenneth Grahame's much-loved 1908 children's classic, *The Wind in the Willows*. The riverside adventures of Ratty, Mole, impulsive Toad and wise old Badger combine idyllic images of boating and picnics with social commentary on a fast-changing world. You can see Badger's cosy parlour, Toad's famous escape from prison disguised as a washerwoman, and the marauding weasels, stoats and ferrets who occupy Toad Hall. Grahame lived for many years by the Thames near Henley and the river runs through his novel as it runs through the town, with their shared love of 'simply messing about in boats'.

An additional treat for visitors is the chance to see close up many of the charming illustrations by E.H. Shepard, one of the best-known illustrators of the famous story.

Above: Ratty and Mole's picnic, a display in The Wind in the Willows exhibition.

Ratty's Refuge

In *The Wind in the Willows*, Ratty was actually a water vole and this garden with its wildlife walkway was designed to celebrate the book's centenary. It provides an important habitat for this endangered species and other wildlife, and is an important and popular educational resource. The garden is based on an award-winning one exhibited by the Museum at the RHS Chelsea Flower Show in 2008.

Above: Ratty's Refuge.

Right: Toad holds forth in this Wind in the Willows exhibit.

A Walk Around Henley

Follow the red route on the map on the back cover to visit some of Henley's highlights. The numbers below correspond with the map key on the inside back cover. The walk is approximately 2 miles (3.5km) long, or for a longer walk it can be extended over the river.

The walk starts and ends at the public car park close to the **River & Rowing Museum** (1). Head towards the river and turn left along the water, passing **Hobbs boat hire** (2).

The brick and timber **Old Granary** (3), on the corner of Thameside and Friday Street, is a reminder that the riverbank would once have been lined with granaries, storing barley and rye for shipping to London. Turn left into picturesque Friday Street, where many of the cottages date from medieval times.

Turn right into Duke Street where you will see the **Tudor House** (5). This street – once a narrow lane with a stream crossing it and nicknamed 'Duck Street' – was the site of a battle during the Civil War. In the 19th century many shops were demolished to make the street wider.

Turn left at the crossroads into **Market Place** (6). The current **Town Hall** (9) (now home to the **Visitor Information Centre**) was built in 1901 in belated celebration of Queen Victoria's Diamond Jubilee.

Above: Friar Park.

It echoes Henley's lovely Georgian houses in the use of red brick, but adds a grand neo-classical pediment.

Walk up Gravel Hill, passing the Old Fire Station, to see **Friar Park** (10). Eccentric London lawyer Frank Crisp commissioned this fantastical castle, completed in 1896. George Harrison, of The Beatles fame, restored the house in the 1970s and his family still live here. It is not open to the public, but visitors can see the elaborate lodge and gateway at the top of the hill. Ancastle Cottage, opposite, was probably a late 16th-century farmhouse.

As you start to head back down into town along West Street, you will see a small, paved public garden where there is a lump of **Ice Age 'pudding stone'** (13). Further along West Street is **The Row Barge** inn (14).

Above: Pub sign in West Street.

Far left: Hobbs of Henley paddle steamer, *The New Orleans*.

Left: Town Hall.

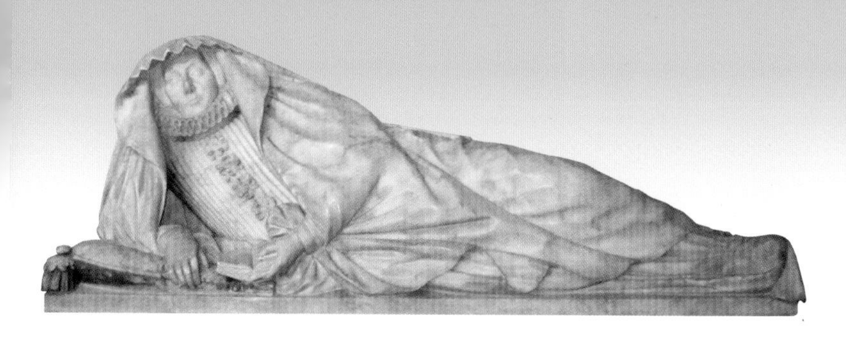

Left: Monument in St Mary's Church.

With the Town Hall on your right, you will see a passageway between the shops that leads to **Kings Arms Barn** (15). This tucked-away building, now offices, is a typical box-framed half-timbered structure, dating from the early 1600s. It was once the stables for the former Kings Arms inn; the last of the Brakspear Brewery dray horses were stabled here until 1947.

At the junction, cross into Hart Street to see **coaching inns** (16), and **Blandy House** (17) on the left. Retrace your steps along Hart Street and turn right into Bell Street where **The Old Bell** inn (19) is on your right – the oldest building in Henley. At **Asquiths** teddy bear shop (20) turn right into New Street with its interesting mix of cottages. Here too are the **Kenton Theatre** (21) the **Rose and Crown** pub (22), the old **brewery** (23) of W.H. Brakspear and Sons and, opposite, the old **malthouse** buildings (24).

Soon after the old brewery buildings, turn right along a narrow pathway; look up to see the ironwork Henley Brewery sign linking the buildings.

Continue into the churchyard, passing the almshouses and the fine, yellow **Chantry House** (27) to reach **St Mary's Church** (28). The Gothic drinking fountain alongside the church commemorates the town's installation of piped water in the 1880s.

King John gave St Mary's to the local lord, Robert de Harcourt, in 1204; its origins date from around AD 1000 and the 13th-century building was restructured over the centuries with medieval stone heads and arches, and a Victorian doorway. A marble monument in the church shows Dame Elizabeth Periam, who founded a school in the Chantry House and died in 1621.

Next to the church is the **Red Lion Hotel** (29) and the handsome **Henley Bridge** (30) which dates from 1786. For a longer walk cross the bridge to take in the sights over the river (see pages 4–5); otherwise turn right at the **Angel on the Bridge** (31) and go back along the riverbank to reach the **River & Rowing Museum** (1) again.

The Museum is one of the town's most significant modern buildings, designed to echo local barns and boathouses. The architects, David Chipperfield, covered a glass and concrete structure in green oak and raised it on columns above the water meadows to combine traditional and modernist forms. With its cafe and interesting exhibitions of local history, the Museum makes a perfect place to end the walk.

Above: Kings Arms Barn.

Above: Red Lion Hotel.

Inns & Breweries

Henley has been rich in pubs since medieval times. The Old Bell on Bell Street dates from 1325, making it the town's oldest surviving house. During the 18th century, Henley's prime position on westward roads from London made it an important stopping place for stagecoaches. By the 1750s there were nearly 40 inns and alehouses.

The well-preserved buildings of the former White Hart Hotel (now a restaurant) housed one of Henley's principal inns, with a 16th-century courtyard where cockfighting and bull baiting used to take place. At busy times, the inn could stable more than 70 horses.

The handsome brick facade of the Red Lion Hotel, which greets visitors crossing Henley Bridge from London, was rebuilt in the 1700s. The White Hart, the Catherine Wheel and others served public coach passengers, but the Red Lion catered for a more exclusive clientele, including the Duke of Marlborough, on his way to Blenheim, and Prince George (later King George IV), who once ate 14 of the inn's celebrated lamb chops at one meal.

Above: Chimney of the old brewery building in New Street.

Above: The old malthouse building in New Street.

Famous Brewers

Henley has been brewing beer for centuries to supply its many inns; with plentiful local barley and running water, the 18th century saw the growth of commercial breweries. Two malting towers and a kiln are still visible behind the building at 18 Hart Street, once home to a wealthy maltster.

Founded in 1779, W.H. Brakspear and Sons was a particularly successful company. The old brewery buildings are in New Street; the malthouse and stables have become flats. In 2002, the brewery moved to Witney where it still brews beer to the traditional 'double drop' method, using the original copper tubs. The seasonal range includes June's floral 'Hooray Henley' and October's fruity 'Henley Bridge'.

The headquarters for the Brakspear chain of pubs is still based in Henley. They run a dedicated Ale Trail every year; collecting a stamp in nine pubs earns drinkers a free pint and a gift.

Henley's traditions live on at Lovibond's Brewery, founded in 2005, behind 19–21 Market Place.

Above: The Angel on the Bridge, with its prime riverside position, dates from 1728.

Below: The Row Barge is one of Henley's ancient coaching inns.

Pubs to Sample

Pub enthusiasts are spoilt for choice in Henley. You could have a pint of Abbot Ale and a tasty meal in The Argyll in Market Place or try the cosy 17th-century Three Tuns which also serves great food and Brakspear beer. You might head up West Street to the spooky Row Barge, with its log fire and suit of armour, or into New Street to try a pudding in the Rose and Crown.

From the historic Angel on the Bridge you can admire the view across the water while sampling one of their fish dishes; alternatively, go on over the bridge to The Little Angel at the end of Remenham Lane, with an enticing menu to suit all tastes.

The Beer Tree on Duke Street has a more modern feel, serving a huge selection of draught and bottled beers alongside traditional and more exotic food. The award-winning Three Horseshoes on Reading Road is a friendly pub in a typical late-Victorian building and the Saracens Head, in Greys Road, is another 'local', with a regular crowd, welcoming open fire and inexpensive bar snacks.

Haunted Henley

An old town always has its fair share of murders, ghost stories and legends. In Henley, almost every building has interesting tales to tell …

Passion and Poison

Half way along Hart Street is a four-storey Grade II listed building known as Blandy House, once home to the Blandy family. In 1751, Mary Blandy murdered her father by putting arsenic in his tea. Francis Blandy, a wealthy lawyer and town clerk, had offered a huge dowry for Mary. Her favourite suitor, Captain Cranston, persuaded her to give her father powders that Cranston said would make Francis kindly disposed to the match. After her father's death, local people chased Mary across the bridge into Berkshire, where she took refuge with the landlady of The Little Angel inn. Mary was hanged at Oxford Castle in 1752.

Bride-and-Seek

A macabre but widespread legend attaches to the 'mistletoe bough chest' at Greys Court manor house near Henley. A young bride hid in the box on her wedding day during a game of hide-and-seek, and then found herself unable to get out. Her body lay undiscovered for several years. The image of a skeleton in bridal wreath and perished silk has led to several ghost stories on this theme.

Above: The mistletoe bough chest at Greys Court.

Stand and Deliver

The flourishing 18th-century stagecoach business drew highwaymen to the tree-covered hills around Henley. The ancient Pack and Prime Lane, now a grassy track leading west out of town, takes its name from this era, when coachmen would pause here to 'pack and prime' their guns. Paranormal investigators have heard the noise of a ghostly horse and carriage on the track.

Above: The Little Angel, one of Mary Blandy's haunts.

Do You Serve Spirits?

Henley's historic coaching inns are riddled with spooky stories. Drinkers have spotted Mary Blandy in The Little Angel, the Catherine Wheel and other pubs. The Row Barge, on West Street, has been an inn for five centuries and reports growling in the cellar, mysterious falling mirrors and slamming doors upstairs. At the Bull Inn on Bell Street, another ancient drinking place, the smell of tallow candles has been noted.

Meanwhile, at nearby Wargrave, a girl who drowned while skating on the frozen river haunts the Thames footpath behind the St George and Dragon.

Films & Books

Henley on Screen

Henley's picturesque riverside and unspoilt neighbouring villages are favourite locations for film and television. Iconic scenes of the Royal Regatta have become significant movie moments, like the Winklevoss twins' rowing race in *The Social Network* (2010). Director David Fincher said: 'I had no idea how huge the Henley Royal Regatta was … this mile-and-a-half of grandstands and corporate sponsors.'

Numerous episodes of *Midsomer Murders* have been filmed in Henley and Hambleden, where at one point the two detectives climb the church tower. The pretty village has also starred in several films over the years, including *Chitty Chitty Bang Bang* (1968).

The lovely house and grounds at Greys Court featured in an episode of the popular TV series *Downton Abbey*, when Greys Court became Downton Place.

Henley also starred in *Bert and Dickie*, a BBC drama first shown in the summer of 2012. It told the tale of two young men in the 1948 London Olympics, who against all odds won gold in the double sculls.

… and in Books

Several famous writers have connections with Henley. Some lived here; others took inspiration from the landscape. The town hosts the Henley Literary Festival in late September, attracting well-known names every year.

The author of *Animal Farm* and *1984*, George Orwell, grew up in Henley and neighbouring Shiplake, and there are plans to create an Orwell centre in a disused chapel. Ian Fleming, who wrote the James Bond books, was also a local boy; his father, Valentine Fleming, was MP for Henley. Creator of Rumpole of the Bailey, John Mortimer, lived in Henley, too, and is buried at St Mary's Church.

The River Thames near Henley helped inspire Kenneth Grahame's much-loved 1908 children's classic, *The Wind in the Willows*. Several grand, riverside houses in the area claim to be the model for Toad Hall, 'a handsome, dignified old house of mellowed red brick'. Fawley Court, a mile north of Henley, is one of many contenders and the Toad Hall Garden Centre in its grounds makes use of the connection.

In Jerome K. Jerome's *Three Men in a Boat*, the three friends moor up on an island near Henley in a wonderful chapter featuring Irish stew and Montmerency's battle with the kettle. Scenes from Charles Dickens' last completed novel, *Our Mutual Friend*, also take place in and near Henley; the victim of an attempted murder on the towpath recovers at an inn, based on the Red Lion.

Above: Spring bedding at Toad Hall Garden Centre.

Left: The church of St Mary the Virgin at Hambleden, dating from the 12th century, has appeared in an episode of *Midsomer Murders*.

Harmonious Henley

With two major music festivals, its own symphony orchestra and connections with famous singers, Henley on Thames is a tuneful town.

Festivals

Henley Festival is a five-night, black-tie extravaganza of music, dance and street theatre in the week after the Regatta, a huge arts' fair and glamorous riverside party, with food, flowers and fireworks. Performers have included Tom Jones, Tim Minchin, Jools Holland, Sting, Blue, Lulu and the Military Wives Choir. From jazz to sculpture, brass bands to cabaret, this annual fixture is as eclectic as it is spectacular.

The Rewind Festival celebrates 80s music over an August weekend in Temple Island Meadows. Previous years have enjoyed acts from Adam Ant, OMD, Kool and the Gang, Marc Almond and numerous other iconic bands and singers. Appealing particularly to people who were teenagers in the 1980s, the festival has become famous for its fun atmosphere.

Local musical talents are showcased in concerts and choral performances of all sorts, including December's Living Advent Calendar, which has involved singers, bellringers, pipers and marching bands. Henley's Youth Festival in March also includes performing arts, with a show at the Kenton Theatre.

Musicians

Beatle George Harrison lived at Friar Park for more than three decades before his death in 2004. He installed a state-of-the-art music studio in the 1970s, known as FPSHOT (Friar Park Studio, Henley on Thames), producing his own albums and others including *Ravi Shankar's Music Festival from India*. Harrison composed *The Ballad of Sir Frankie Crisp (Let it Roll)* in memory of the house's original owner.

The singer Dusty Springfield, famous for songs like *Son of a Preacher Man* and *I Only Want to Be With You*, also spent her last years in Henley on Thames. Her funeral took place in St Mary's Church, where some of her ashes are buried; fans continue to put flowers on her memorial in the graveyard here.

Above: Henley's retro Rewind Festival was first held in 2009.

Left: The Henley Festival offers music of all genres, plus comedy, dance, street theatre and the most spectacular firework displays.

Theatre, Art & Design

Henley's Kenton Theatre is the fourth-oldest working theatre in Britain, housed in an elegant Georgian building which opened in 1805. Local artist John Piper helped to restore the theatre in 1951 and painted the proscenium arch.

John Piper (1903–92) was a painter and printmaker who lived in the tiny village of Fawley Bottom, north of Henley. He was an official war artist during the Second World War and designed stained glass for Coventry's new cathedral after the Blitz. The River & Rowing Museum has examples of his work, including ceramics, stage designs, book covers and murals.

The 18th-century sculptor Anne Damer carved the heads of Tamesis and Isis, which decorate Henley Bridge. Damer grew up at Park Place; her father, Henry Seymour Conway, was a Field-Marshal and influential landowner.

Humphrey Gainsborough, a local dissenting clergyman and engineer, designed Marsh Lock. He was a prolific inventor, winning a prize for his drill plough and developing a steam engine. A blue plaque marks the site of his chapel near Christ Church on Reading Road, not far from Henley station; his brother was the painter Thomas Gainsborough.

Henley's modern sculptures include Sean Henry's painted bronze figures of Olympic rowers Steven Redgrave and Matthew Pinsent (2002) outside the River & Rowing Museum. The sportsmen are facing the Thames, where they trained, and are depicted holding oars and ready to take to the water.

The town has an extraordinary number of art galleries, whose colourful windows brighten the streets, and more than 150 local artists exhibit their work at a range of venues on the Henley Art Trail in May.

Above: The carved head of Tamesis on Henley Bridge.

Right: The 'Green Man' plate designed by John Piper for Wedgwood.

Left: Bronze sculpture of Steve Redgrave and Matthew Pinsent.

Left: Blue plaque to Humphrey Gainsborough on Reading Road.

Food, Drink & Shopping

Above: Market Place from the Town Hall.

As well as some delightful pubs, Henley has much to offer in the way of refreshment with a good selection of cafes and restaurants, and great shops too.

Alongside lovely art galleries and boutiques, there are dozens of quirky stores selling everything from souvenir teddy bears at Asquiths in New Street to first editions of *Casino Royale* at Jonker's Rare Books on Hart Street. Artist Simon Drew was born in nearby Caversham and has a shop dedicated to his work in New Street. Antiques and vintage items are a Henley speciality; Tudor House on Duke Street is one of many Aladdin's caves of curious and forgotten treasures.

Henley's historic market still runs every Thursday, selling local crafts and produce. Many things have been made in Henley over the centuries, from bricks and glass to beer and sausages; industries change, but local businesses still thrive.

Software engineer-turned-brewer Jeff Rosenmeier is continuing Henley's historic traditions at Lovibonds, on the site of an older brewery behind Market Place; the beer garden has a narrow gauge track from the previous business. Visitors can taste 'Henley Gold' or 'Henley Dark', made from malted barley which is smoked using Chiltern beechwood.

Round the corner, there has been a butcher's shop in the half-timbered house at 7 Market Place since 1861. Gabriel Machin sells all kinds of delicacies from home-smoked salmon and locally sourced game to Mapledurham Mill's stone-ground flour.

Henley is heaven if you have a sweet tooth. Leanne Herbert's Cakepop Company makes delicious buttercream truffle cakes, while Gorvett and Stone serve handmade chocolates in their shop on Duke Street, including cinder toffee made with local honey. Imaginative sugar craft is also on show on the celebration cakes a few doors down at Confetti and Spice.

Organic baby-food producer Ella's Kitchen has its headquarters in a barn near Henley at Rotherfield Greys. Ella's all-fruit smoothies in bright pouches have become super-popular with parents in several countries since Paul Lindley founded the company in 2006.

Left: Asquiths sell every type of teddy bear imaginable.

In & Around Henley

Places to Visit

Stonor Park

The manor house at Stonor, 5 miles (8km) north of Henley, has been home to the Stonor family for over 850 years and is now home to The Lord and Lady Camoys. The history of the house inevitably contributes to the atmosphere, unpretentious yet grand. A facade of warm brick with Georgian windows conceals older buildings dating back to the 12th century, and a 14th-century Catholic chapel sits on the south-east corner. Mass has been celebrated here since medieval times.

Stonor nestles in a fold of the beautiful wooded Chiltern Hills with breathtaking views of the park (accessible by public footpath all year round), where fallow deer have grazed for centuries. The gardens offer outstanding views of the park, and are especially beautiful in May and June, containing fine displays of irises, peonies, lavenders and roses along with other herbaceous plants and shrubs.

The house, with its collections of art and ceramics, Venetian globes, French wallpaper and family portraits, is open on Sunday afternoons from April to September, and Wednesday afternoons during July and August, along with the gardens, and there is a tearoom in the Old Hall.

Above: Nuffield Place, home of the founder of Morris Motor Cars.

Nuffield Place

The National Trust has opened and is restoring Nuffield Place at Huntercombe (7 miles/11km north-west of Henley), home of William Morris, founder of Morris Motor Cars. He bought the house in 1933 and his pipes and porcelain, cartoons and cocktail cabinet are preserved in the comfortable, 'time capsule' interiors. The philanthropic Morris (Lord Nuffield) started out repairing bicycles in the 1890s; visitors can see the life-saving iron lung he invented, the tool cupboard in his bedroom, and the cars he drove. Beech woods surround the lovely gardens and vintage cafe.

Below: The manor house at Stonor Park.

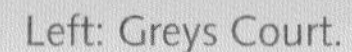

Left: Greys Court.

Greys Court

The National Trust property at Greys Court, 3 miles (5km) west of Henley, makes an interesting outing. The De Grey family fortified it in the 14th century; the Brunners restored it in the 1930s, and the intervening owners (including – briefly – Ian Fleming's mother) created a jumble of wood and stone, brick and flint. In summer the gardens are bright with roses, clematis, columbines and ancient wisteria. Inside the house are stained-glass windows, wreaths of plaster flowers and theatrical relics like daggers from Henry Irving's famous portrayal of Macbeth.

Visitors can walk from Henley to Greys Court along a grassy valley; those who arrive on foot or by bus are entitled to a free cup of tea in the tearoom! The woods along the route are especially pretty in spring, with a carpet of bluebells, and autumn, when the Chiltern beeches turn copper and gold.

Warburg Nature Reserve

This 265 acre (107ha) nature reserve, 4 miles (6.5km) north-west of Henley, is the best Berks, Bucks and Oxon Wildlife Trust reserve for orchids, where 15 species flower from April to August. Take your binoculars and stroll among the beautiful Chiltern woodland and grassland to spot hosts of butterflies, birds and flowers.

Harpsden

Pre-Roman coins have been found at Harpsden, a mile (1.5km) south of Henley, and the privately owned manor house here, a popular film location, is listed in the Domesday Book. Two old barns near Harpsden Court are decorated with carved wooden blocks, originally made for printing wallpaper.

Rotherfield Greys

In this pretty village, 3 miles (5km) from Henley, St Nicholas' Church has a 14th-century brass memorial to Sir Robert de Grey and alabaster figures in the Knollys Chapel.

Park Place

Although not open to the public, a mile (1.5km) from the town is the privately owned Park Place, on the hill above Marsh Lock. It was built in 1720 in the style of a French chateau and Humphrey Gainsborough was employed to make a rustic bridge across the valley. The grounds, which also contain a 'Druids Temple', a gabled boathouse and other landscape features, inspired the Lost Gardens of Heligan in Cornwall.

Above: Warburg Nature Reserve.